weird but true! 9

350 OUTRAGEOUS FACTS

NATIONAL GEOGRAPHIC
WASHINGTON, D.C.

4

The planet Venus may have once been habitable.

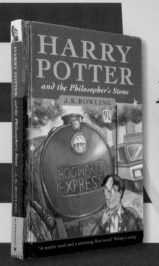

Some **500** first-edition copies of **Harry Potter and the Philosopher's Stone** were printed with a **typo**—and are now worth tens of thousands of dollars.

A SCIENTIST IN MEXICO HAS DEVELOPED THE TECHNOLOGY TO CREATE **GLOW-IN-THE-DARK** SIDEWALKS.

AN ARTIST USED **NESTS** FROM **WASPS AND HORNETS TO** CREATE A HUMAN-SIZE **SCULPTURE OF A QUEEN BEE.**

Some types of **algae** eat themselves when food is scarce.

SOUTH AMERICAN

ANTS

HAVE BEEN

FARMING

FUNGI FOR

6o MILLION YEARS.

7

WHITE ADMIRAL BUTTERFLY POOP SMELLS LIKE MINT.

The second **new moon** in a **month** is called a **black moon.**

A BLACK MOON OCCURS ONLY ABOUT ONCE EVERY 32 MONTHS.

Some **mosquitoes** prefer **cow blood** to **human blood.**

A **spider** in Australia breathes **underwater** and eats **toads.**

GULP!

9

Scientists have figured out how to...

...turn rotten **tomatoes** into **energy.**

boo!

...turn rats **transparent.**

...turn plastic trash into **fuel.**

...make a substance similar to **kryptonite.**

...create a **battery** inspired by **vitamins.**

...make a toilet that can **generate electricity** from **urine.**

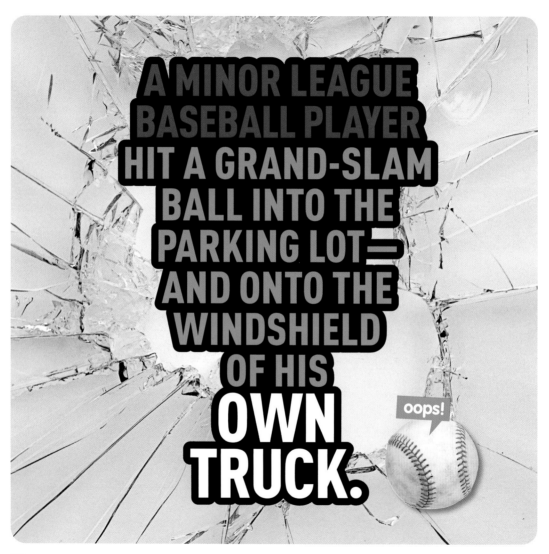

A MINOR LEAGUE BASEBALL PLAYER HIT A GRAND-SLAM BALL INTO THE PARKING LOT AND ONTO THE WINDSHIELD OF HIS OWN TRUCK.

oops!

The **metal** in one of **King Tut's daggers** was made using **iron** from a **meteorite.**

A COMPANY IN SPAIN **DEVELOPED A 3-D PRINTER** THAT CAN MAKE **PIZZA.**

TWO TEENAGERS IN WISCONSIN, U.S.A., BUILT A BACKYARD ROLLER COASTER.

A **pair of birds** in Angus, Scotland, regularly **steal underwear and socks** from swimmers.

The world's first year-round ice hotel opened in Sweden.

There are 130 species of fish that spend at least some of their time on dry land.

THE MANCHINEEL TREE IS SO **TOXIC** THAT EVEN STANDING UNDER IT IN RAINY WEATHER IS DANGEROUS.

OLYMPIC GOLD MEDALS ARE WORTH AROUND $600.

You can **swim** as fast in **syrup** as you can in **water.**

A GIANT INFLATABLE MOON ROLLED OVER TRAFFIC ON A BUSY HIGHWAY IN CHINA.

The **town** of Codell, Kansas, U.S.A., was hit by a **tornado** on **May 20** in **1916, 1917,** and **1918.**

SCIENTISTS RECENTLY DISCOVERED A PREHISTORIC **SCORPION** THAT GREW AS LONG AS **A HUMAN.**

Scientists put **fitness-tracking** technology on **squirrels** to see how much **energy** they used.

SOME FLOWER ARRANGEMENTS IN VICTORIAN ENGLAND CONTAINED CODED MESSAGES.

GORiLLAS SOMETIMES SING HAPPY SONGS WHEN THEY EAT.

23

A hotel straddling the border of France and Switzerland lets you sleep with **your head** in one country and **your feet** in the other.

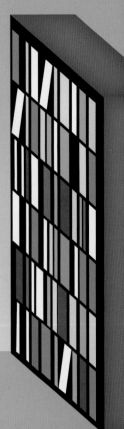

THE U.S.-CANADIAN BORDER RUNS THROUGH THE MIDDLE OF A LIBRARY.

Some **scientists** think that most of the **universe** is trapped inside **ancient black holes.**

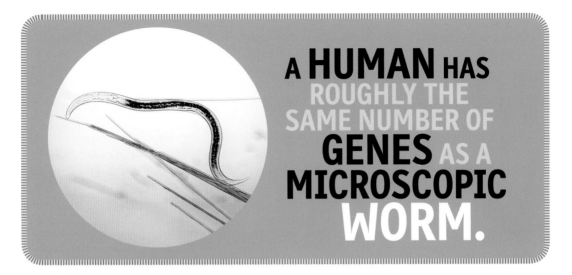

A **HUMAN** HAS ROUGHLY THE SAME NUMBER OF **GENES** AS A **MICROSCOPIC WORM.**

SCIENTISTS HAVE ENGINEERED **SPINACH** PLANTS THAT CAN **DETECT BOMBS.**

Every August, people in Bolivia gather to **break rocks** for **good luck.**

Sociable
weavers
build
"apartment"
nests that can
house up to
500
birds.

THE COMMUNAL **NESTS** CAN **WEIGH** AS MUCH AS A SMALL **CAR.**

A BILLIONAIRE BOUGHT **EIGHT** $1,000 SMARTPHONES— FOR HIS **DOG.**

A whooping crane's eyes change from blue to aqua to *gold* as it grows older.

Thieves in Wisconsin, U.S.A., stole 20,000 pounds (9,072 kg) of cheese.

SCIENTISTS USED BACTERIA TO MAKE A MICROSCOPIC WIND FARM.

There are decomposed **wasps** inside of figs.

Flat millipedes shoot a defensive spray that smells like cherry cola.

33

THERE'S A SCULPTURE AS TALL AS A GIRAFFE SITTING ON THE OCEAN FLOOR IN THE BAHAMAS.

MOTHS ARE EVOLVING TO BE LESS ATTRACTED TO LIGHT.

A CITY IN GERMANY INSTALLED **TRAFFIC SIGNALS** ON ITS **SIDEWALKS.**

A New York City **museum** offered visitors the chance to use an **18-karat-gold toilet.**

THE CONTINENT OF AUSTRALIA MOVES BACK AND FORTH WHEN THE SEASONS CHANGE.

AUSTRALIA HAS DRIFTED ALMOST FIVE FEET (1.5 m) NORTH IN THE PAST 22 YEARS.

IN TAIWAN, IT'S TRENDY TO GET YOUR **DOG'S FUR** GROOMED INTO **GEOMETRIC SHAPES.**

38

COFFEE JELLY— A JIGGLY DESSERT MADE FROM **ESPRESSO—** IS A POPULAR **DESSERT** IN JAPAN.

BLACK HOLES "EAT" STARS AND "BURP" GAS.

Researchers observed a **sea lion** named **Ronan** bobbing her head in time with **music.**

40

41

Leonardo da Vinci may have written backward

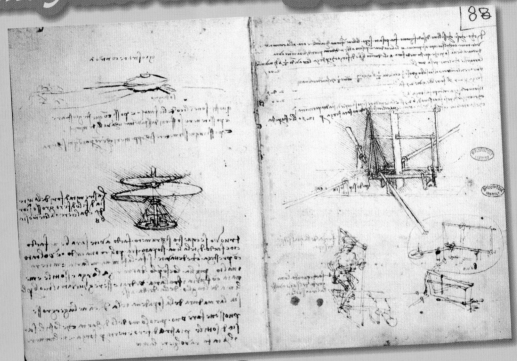

88

to keep people from stealing his ideas.

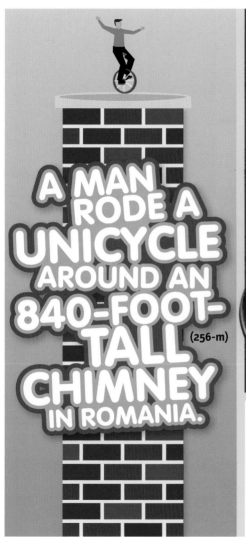

A MAN RODE A UNICYCLE AROUND AN 840-FOOT-TALL (256-m) CHIMNEY IN ROMANIA.

Chork=
chopsticks + fork

A man accidentally discovered a **49,000-year-old** human settlement while taking a **bathroom break** in an Australian park.

Parts of the Great Wall of China are **STILL BEING DISCOVERED.**

In just two days, AMATEUR ASTRONOMERS found more than **80** NEW PLANETS outside our solar system.

One of the planets has **FOUR SUNS.**

A Chihuahua named Miracle Milly holds the world record for **SHORTEST DOG: 3.8** (9.65 cm) INCHES TALL.

90-YEAR-OLD mold sold for $14,617.

In 2017, a **70-YEAR-OLD** woman ran **7 MARATHONS** on **7 CONTINENTS** in **7 DAYS.**

NASA once paid a man **$18,000** to lie in bed for **70 DAYS.**

VIDEO GAMES could help treat **DEPRESSION,** ONE STUDY FOUND.

Zookeepers in Washington, D.C., U.S.A., once **SHIPPED A GIANT PANDA** to his new home in China.

You use **200** MUSCLES to take **one step.**

A male **BABIRUSA'S TUSKS** can grow long enough to **CURL BACK** and pierce the animal's skull.

Ancient Romans carried **PORTABLE SUNDIALS** for telling time on the go.

That's Weird!

KOALAS can **sleep** **22** HOURS A DAY.

The pop-up **Museum** of **Ice Cream** in New York City featured a swimmable **pool** full of faux rainbow sprinkles.

 **DRAGONFLIES CAN LIVE UNDERWATER FOR TWO YEARS.**

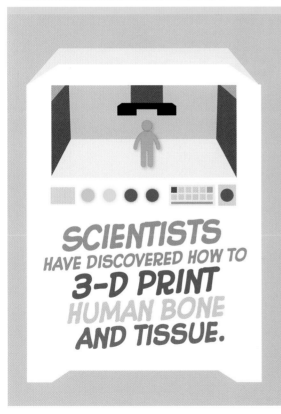

SCIENTISTS HAVE DISCOVERED HOW TO **3-D PRINT** HUMAN BONE AND TISSUE.

THERE ARE AS MANY STRANDS OF CORN SILK AS THERE ARE KERNELS ON THE COB.

A family in New Jersey, U.S.A., lives in a farmhouse encased in an aircraft hangar.

FRESHWATER SNAILS KILL MORE HUMANS EVERY YEAR THAN DO LIONS, WOLVES, CROCODILES, AND SHARKS COMBINED.

Some piranhas are vegetarian.

THE LAWS OF PHYSICS DO NOT RULE OUT TIME TRAVEL.

You can buy a **smartphone case** that **looks like an ice-cream sandwich.**

Early ketchup recipes included mushrooms, oysters, and walnuts— but no tomatoes.

A NEW SPECIES OF **TROPICAL ANT** WAS RECENTLY **DISCOVERED IN A FROG'S BELLY.**

It costs the **U.S. Mint** about **eight cents** to make **one nickel.**

Benjamin Franklin invented a glass harmonica.

THE FIRST ANIMALS LAUNCHED INTO OUTER SPACE?

FRUIT FLIES.

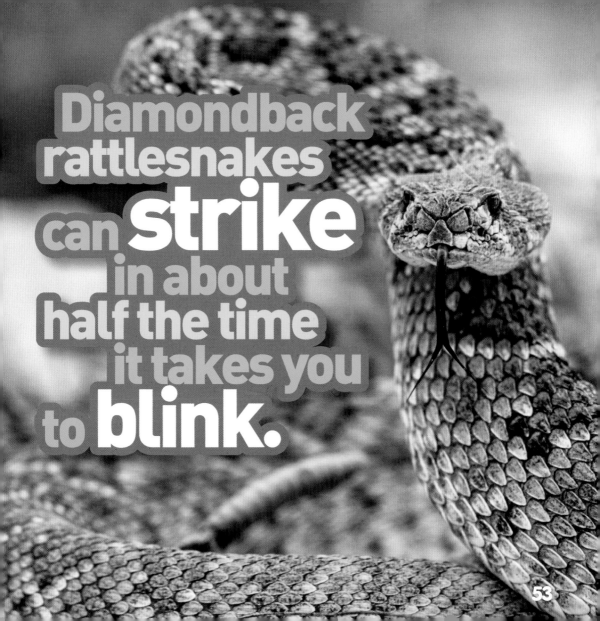

Diamondback rattlesnakes can **strike** in about half the time it takes you to **blink.**

An **artist** created the world's largest **biodegradable portrait** on a grassy slope in Switzerland.

Scientists recently discovered a glowing purple blob on the floor of the Pacific Ocean.

A FAST-FOOD RESTAURANT ONCE GAVE AWAY FRIED-CHICKEN-SCENTED SUNSCREEN.

A 31-YEAR-OLD **CRIMINAL** WAS ABLE TO EVADE **POLICE** FOR MONTHS BY DISGUISING HIMSELF **AS AN OLD MAN.**

THE **U.S.** STATES OF ALASKA AND HAWAII HAVE THE SAME RECORD-HIGH TEMPERATURE: 100°F.

(37.8°C)

AN **ARTIST** IN PHILADELPHIA, PENNSYLVANIA, U.S.A., CREATES **ART** USING DISCARDED **CANDY WRAPPERS.**

COCKROACHES ARE MORE LIKELY TO FLY IN HOT WEATHER.

MILK

ONE PINT (473mL)

60

THE PACIFIC BEETLE COCKROACH

HEY, GUYS, WAIT UP!

Cockroaches
have a built-in GPS!

PRODUCES MILK.

COCKROACH MILK IS MORE NUTRITIOUS THAN COW'S MILK.

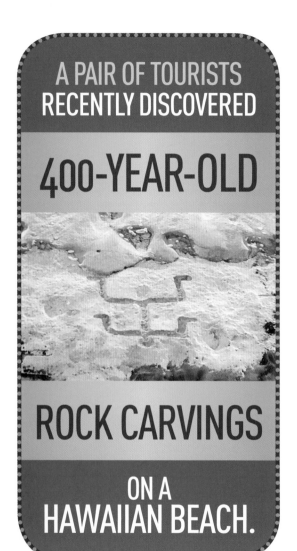

A PAIR OF TOURISTS RECENTLY DISCOVERED

400-YEAR-OLD

ROCK CARVINGS

ON A HAWAIIAN BEACH.

It was once believed that massaging ground-up **pumpkin** onto your face could remove **freckles.**

A man in New York, U.S.A., returned a **library book** that was **15,531 days** (that's 42 years!) **overdue.**

DIVERS EXPLORING A SHIPWRECK OFF THE COAST OF SWEDEN FOUND A HUNK OF 340-YEAR-OLD CHEESE INSIDE A SEALED CONTAINER.

The oldest known **orca**— nicknamed "Granny"— lived to be 105.

Firefighting was an unofficial event at the 1900 Summer Olympics in Paris, France.

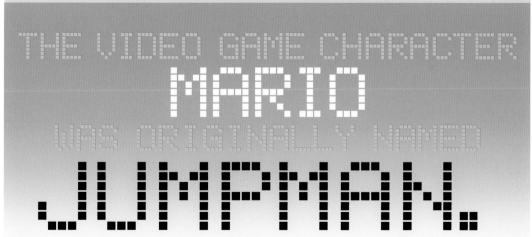

THE VIDEO GAME CHARACTER **MARIO** WAS ORIGINALLY NAMED **JUMPMAN.**

MINIATURE BLACK HOLES MAY BE

PASSING THROUGH EARTH EVERY DAY, A STUDY FOUND.

TEN PERCENT OF THE WORLD'S REDHEADS LIVE IN IRELAND.

Ireland is about the size of **South Carolina, U.S.A.**

A **1,075-year-old pine tree** in Greece is the oldest known living thing in Europe.

SOME RATTLESNAKES IN THE GRAND CANYON ARE PINK.

A mouse scurrying through displays at the Museum of English Rural Life in Great Britain got caught in a 155-year-old mousetrap.

SEA STARS DON'T HAVE BLOOD.

Great frigate birds can fly for two months straight without landing.

THEY **NAP** WHILE THEY'RE FLYING.

SCIENTISTS THINK THAT BOTH **REPTILES** AND **BIRDS** MAY **DREAM** WHILE SLEEPING.

THE EARTH'S SURFACE IS TWO AND A HALF YEARS OLDER THAN ITS CORE.

Paramedics in Connecticut, U.S.A., came to a **squirrel's rescue** after its **head became stuck** in a **yogurt container.**

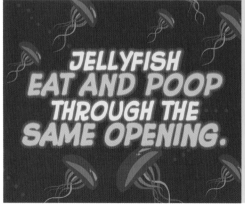

JELLYFISH EAT AND POOP THROUGH THE SAME OPENING.

A **bakery** in London sells a **doughnut** topped with caviar, gold leaf, gold vanilla beans, and a rare type of chocolate. **The price tag?** £1,500, or about $2,000.

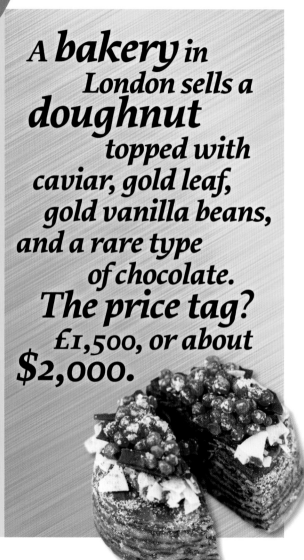

A friendly **stray dog** followed an **ultramarathon runner** for **77 miles** (124 km) in China's Gobi desert.

HOW'S MY PACE?

Chameleon spit is 400 times thicker than human spit.

CHAMELEONS' **TOES** ARE FUSED TOGETHER IN GROUPS OF TWOS AND THREES.

A NEW YORK RESTAURANT
SERVES PIZZA
IN A BOX

MADE OF PIZZA.

SCIENTISTS USED A
3-D PRINTER TO MAKE
A PROSTHETIC BEAK
FOR A GOOSE MISSING MOST OF HER BILL.

When a **bee stings,**
it releases a chemical
that smells like
bananas.

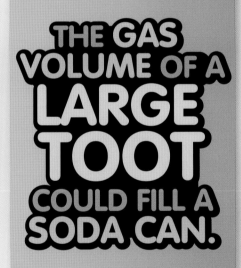

THE GAS VOLUME OF A **LARGE TOOT** COULD FILL A SODA CAN.

Underwater **volcanoes** cover more of the **Earth** than deserts or tundras.

THREE-TOED SLOTHS
BURN ONLY
110 CALORIES
A DAY—
ABOUT THE SAME AS A
HUMAN PLAYING SOCCER
FOR 10 MINUTES.

IO, A MOON OF JUPITER, HAS **VOLCANOES** THAT BLAST **310** MILES (500 km) INTO SPACE.

OCTOPUSES CAN EDIT THEIR OWN **GENES.**

Scientists grew **CHICKEN MEAT** in a lab.

PEOPLE WHO HAVE THE LENSES OF THEIR EYES REMOVED CAN SEE ULTRAVIOLET LIGHT.

A 1953 letter from **ALBERT EINSTEIN** to a science teacher sold at an auction for **$53,503.75.**

A RUSSIAN COMPANY CREATED THE WORLDS' FIRST **RIDEABLE HOVERBIKE.**

Screech owls **BRING SNAKES** back to their nests to keep them **PEST FREE.**

An elephant in South Korea can **IMITATE HUMAN SPEECH.**

SPIDERS consume as much MEAT ANNUALLY as all 7 BILLION HUMANS on Earth do.

A wall in Paris is covered with the words **"I LOVE YOU"** in **250** languages.

California ground squirrels have been observed **BITING** and **THROWING PEBBLES** at rattlesnakes.

That's Weird!

Adult cats **MEOW** only at **humans,** not at **EACH OTHER.**

86

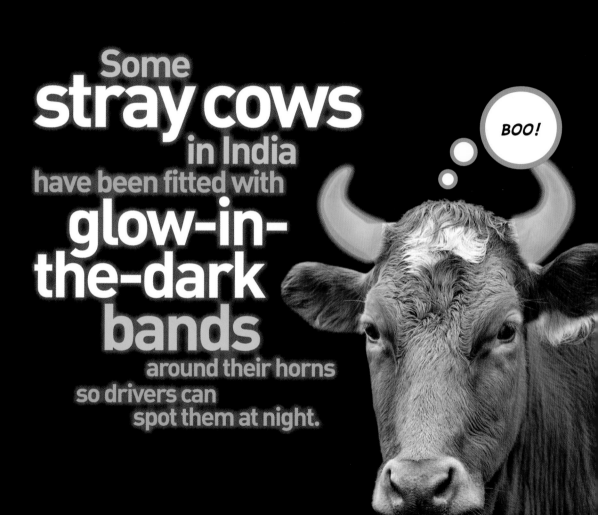

PARTS OF **BEIJING, CHINA,** ARE **SINKING** BY UP TO **FOUR** INCHES (10.2 cm) A YEAR, A STUDY SHOWED.

Most **kangaroos** are left-handed.

MILLIONS OF MOSQUITOES CAN FORM TWISTING, TORNADO-LIKE SWARMS THAT CAN REACH UP TO 1,000 (305 m) FEET TALL.

JANUARY 14 IS
DRESS UP
YOUR PET DAY.

NEVER FORCE YOUR
PET TO DO OR WEAR
ANYTHING IT
DOESN'T WANT TO.

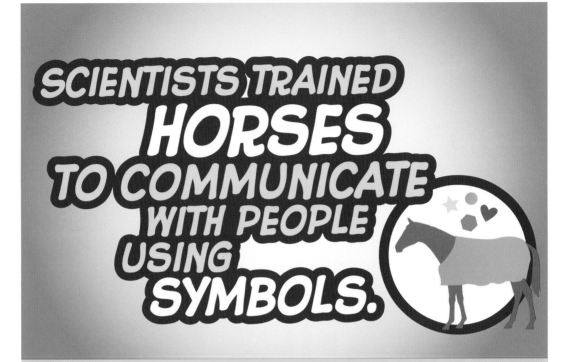

SCIENTISTS TRAINED **HORSES** TO COMMUNICATE WITH PEOPLE USING SYMBOLS.

HORSE HOOVES NEVER STOP GROWING.

OOH, A WARM SPOT!

FISH **PEE** HELPS

CORAL REEFS THRIVE.

An **alligator** was seen using **a crosswalk** in northern Florida, U.S.A.

IS THERE A PROBLEM, OFFICER?

GUINEA PIGS OFTEN SLEEP WITH THEIR EYES OPEN.

PLAYING 3-D VIDEO GAMES CAN IMPROVE YOUR MEMORY, A STUDY FOUND.

DØDSING=
BELLY FLOPPING OFF A THREE-STORY-TALL PLATFORM

IT HAS SNOWED IN THE SAHARA.

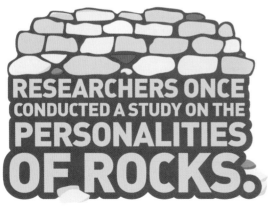

RESEARCHERS ONCE CONDUCTED A STUDY ON THE PERSONALITIES OF ROCKS.

Toads don't have teeth (but frogs do).

A **mama moose** **gave birth to a calf** in a **shopping center** parking lot in Anchorage, Alaska, U.S.A.

www.bigidahopotato.com

A BIG HELPING

The Famous Idaho Potato Tour

YOU'LL KNOW IT'S REAL
When You See the Seal!

A SIX-TON (5.4-t) "POTATO" FLOATED ON A BARGE ALONG A RIVER IN NEW YORK, U.S.A.

DID SOMEONE SAY FRENCH FRIES?

www.bigidahopotato.com

OVERSIZE LOAD

A REAL POTATO THAT SIZE COULD MAKE 1.5 MILLION FRENCH FRIES.

You can go to elf school in Reykjavík, Iceland.

0.001 PERCENT OF YOUR TAN COMES FROM PHOTONS LEFT OVER FROM THE BIG BANG.

The Royal Norwegian Guard promoted a **penguin** named **Sir Nils Olav III** to **brigadier,** one of its highest honors.

Invisible poems
were painted on
sidewalks
in Boston, Massachusetts, U.S.A.

MY HOPES THE

SNOW H

LOOKS LIKE BETWEEN 'EM THEY DONE

TRIED TO MAKE ME

STOP LAUGHIN' STOP LOVIN' STOP LIVIN
BUT I DON'T CARE!
I'M STILL HERE!

N HU

YOU CAN SEE THEM ONLY WHEN THE GROUND GETS WET.

The Eiffel Tower seems smaller if you lean left while looking at it.

FARMERS IN SUNDERLAND, MASSACHUSETTS, U.S.A., DESIGNED A CORN MAZE INSPIRED BY THE NOVEL ALICE'S ADVENTURES IN WONDERLAND.

TEETH

CAN GROW ANYWHERE THROUGHOUT THE BODY—INCLUDING INSIDE YOUR

NOSE.

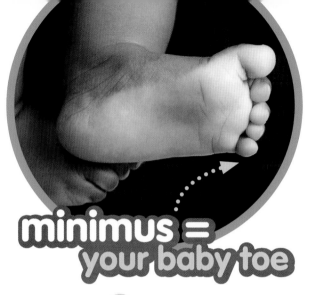

minimus = your baby toe

pinna = the outer part of your ear

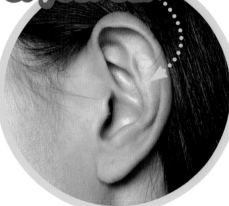

purlicue = the space between your thumb and forefinger

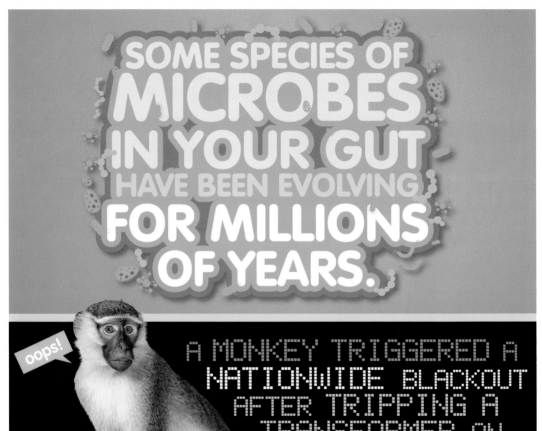

SOME SPECIES OF **MICROBES** IN YOUR GUT HAVE BEEN EVOLVING **FOR MILLIONS OF YEARS.**

oops!

A MONKEY TRIGGERED A NATIONWIDE BLACKOUT AFTER TRIPPING A TRANSFORMER ON THE ROOF OF A POWER PLANT IN KENYA.

A ranch in Texas, U.S.A., is two-thirds the size of Rhode Island.

YOU CAN BUY **FRESH EGGS** FROM **VENDING MACHINES** IN JAPAN.

A **DOG** NAMED **DUKE** WAS ELECTED **MAYOR OF CORMORANT,** MINNESOTA, U.S.A.

109

Scientists use rainbows to study air pollution.

One hundred years ago, New York City **taxi cabs** were painted **green and red**, not **yellow.**

SWEET TREATS

MAKE BEES FEEL

OPTIMISTIC,

ONE STUDY FOUND.

A MAN DRESSED AS **DARTH VADER** WAS SPOTTED PICKING UP **TRASH** ALONGSIDE A HIGHWAY IN VIRGINIA, U.S.A.

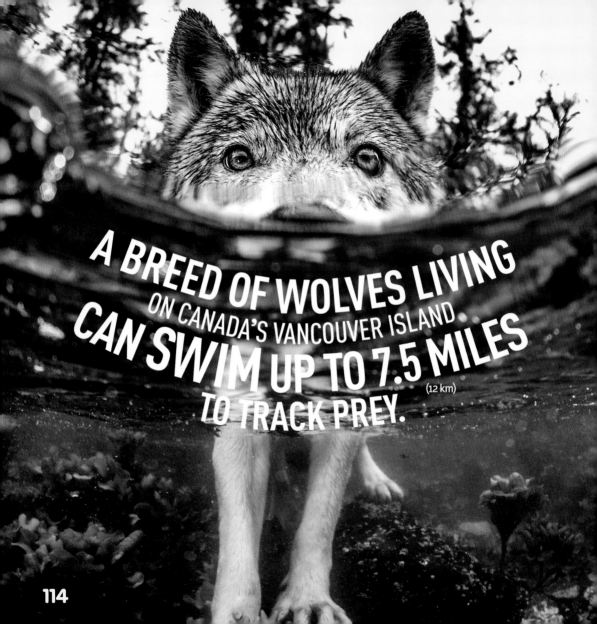

A BREED OF WOLVES LIVING
ON CANADA'S VANCOUVER ISLAND
CAN SWIM UP TO 7.5 MILES
(12 km)
TO TRACK PREY.

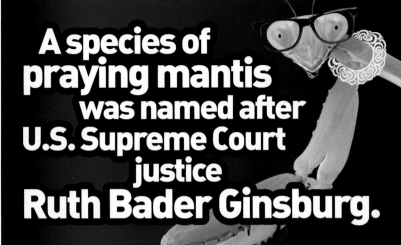

A species of praying mantis was named after U.S. Supreme Court justice Ruth Bader Ginsburg.

A popular fast-food restaurant in India sells chicken inside a container that can charge your cell phone.

FRUIT FLIES CAN SUFFER FROM INSOMNIA.

Yawning

may help
cool
your brain.

ANIMALS WITH **LARGE** BRAINS YAWN LONGER THAN ANIMALS WITH **SMALL** BRAINS.

A **BEAR** IN NEW MEXICO, U.S.A., **HITCHED A RIDE** ON TOP OF A **GARBAGE TRUCK** FOR **FIVE MILES** BEFORE CLIMBING OFF.
(8 km)

During the **world's longest race,** runners cover almost **60 miles** (97 km) **a day for 52 days.**

A small swimming snail known as a **sea butterfly** flaps its tiny wings to move through the water.

snotbot=
A ROBOT THAT COLLECTS WHALE SNOT FOR STUDY

A BLUE HOLE NEARLY AS DEEP AS THE HEIGHT OF THE EMPIRE STATE BUILDING

WAS RECENTLY DISCOVERED IN THE SOUTH CHINA SEA.

MOST ANIMALS DON'T CHEW THEIR FOOD.

A GERMAN COMPANY INVENTED **A ROBOTIC OCTOPUS-LIKE TENTACLE** THAT CAN **WRAP** AROUND OBJECTS AND PICK THEM UP.

SCIENTISTS ARE WORKING ON MAKING A **FABRIC OUT OF HAGFISH SLIME.**

ONE SPECIES OF CRAB LIVES IN TREES.

A PRINCE FROM SAUDI ARABIA ONCE BROUGHT **80 BIRDS** OF PREY WITH HIM ON A PLANE.

Each bird got its own seat.

SCIENTISTS INVENTED A SMARTPHONE SCREEN MATERIAL **THAT CAN REPAIR ITSELF** FROM CUTS AND SCRATCHES.

A scientist found an ancient fossilized tick filled with **20-MILLION-YEAR-OLD** MAMMAL BLOOD.

SCIENTISTS DISCOVERED 13,000-YEAR-OLD human teeth with fillings made of ingredients like plant fiber and hair.

124

DOLPHINS IN AUSTRALIA HAVE BEEN OBSERVED **TOSSING OCTOPUSES** BEFORE EATING THEM TO "TENDERIZE" THEM.

LEATHERBACK TURTLES EAT ALMOST NOTHING **BESIDES JELLYFISH.**

Scientists developed an experimental system that **allowed a paralyzed** man to control his arm and **hand with his thoughts.**

A cockatiel named **COCO** can **SING OPERA.**

SEA-DWELLING WORM SNAILS SHOOT OUT A **WEB OF MUCUS FROM THEIR TENTACLES** TO TRAP PREY.

That's Weird!

CHINA PLANS TO OPEN THE WORLD'S FIRST **PANDA RETIREMENT HOME.**

SCOTLAND'S NATIONAL ANIMAL IS A UNICORN.

According to researchers in Australia, **eating bananas** can make **human toots** less smelly.

petrichor = the smell in the **air** following **rain**

DON'T TRY THIS AT HOME!

One **summer,** residents of **Philadelphia,** Pennsylvania, U.S.A., swam in Dumpster **"pools"** to beat the heat.

127

CHICKENS ARE GENETICALLY CLOSER TO DINOSAURS THAN THEY ARE TO OTHER BIRDS.

Pacu fish crack open seeds and nuts with their humanlike teeth.

128

SEABIRD POOP HELPS KEEP THE ARCTIC CLIMATE **COOL.**

Tossing a **ball** of **aluminum foil** in your dryer can fight **static electricity.**

A *suit of armor* *for a* *guinea pig—* *complete with a* *jacket and tiny helmet—* *sold online* *for more than* **$24,000.**

A SINGLE LAKE IN SIBERIA CONTAINS ONE-FIFTH OF ALL THE FRESHWATER IN THE WORLD.

A **giraffe** can clean its **nose** with its **tongue.**

THE LONGEST-LASTING LIGHTNING BOLT EVER RECORDED WAS 7.74 SECONDS.

SPIDERS HEAR WITH THEIR LEGS.

A chef in New York City created a **doughnut** made from **purple yams** and dipped in **edible gold.**

A NEW NATION CALLED **ASGARDIA** HAS BEEN ESTABLISHED IN OUTER SPACE.

RESEARCHERS RECENTLY FOUND INTACT **2,000-**YEAR-OLD **HUMAN REMAINS** ON A **SHIPWRECK** OFF THE COAST OF **GREECE.**

AT BIRTH, A GIANT PACIFIC OCTOPUS IS ABOUT THE SIZE OF A MOSQUITO.

The smallest mammal ever—**a prehistoric rodent**—was as big as your fingernail and weighed no more than a dollar bill.

Baby **jackals** eat their parents' **vomit.**

137

THE FOREST CANOPY IN THE AMAZON IS SO THICK

THAT IT CAN TAKE **10 MINUTES** FOR RAIN TO REACH FROM THE TOP OF THE TREES TO **THE GROUND.**

THE BLUE COLOR USED IN JEANS MAY DATE BACK 6,000 YEARS.

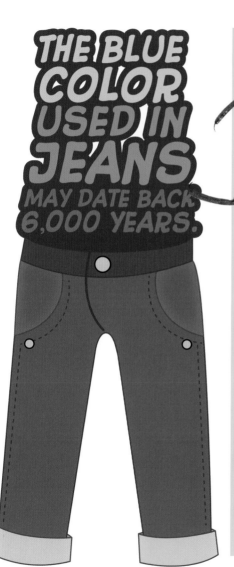

A WATER BUG NATIVE TO SOUTHEAST ASIA

CAN GROW AS BIG AS YOUR PALM.

A CHICKEN NAMED PATRICK PLAYS THE PIANO BY PECKING THE KEYS WITH HIS BEAK.

A HONEYBEE CAN LIFT ABOUT
80 PERCENT OF ITS
BODY WEIGHT IN POLLEN.

WHALES CAN TASTE ONLY SALTY FOODS.

142

Some **hermit crabs** use discarded **trash** as shells.

Residents of Green Bank, West Virginia, U.S.A., can't use **Wi-Fi** because of a **high-tech** government **telescope** located there.

RADIOS AND CELL PHONES ARE ALSO **BANNED.**

144

TURTLES MAY HAVE FIRST EVOLVED SHELLS TO HELP THEM BURROW INTO THE EARTH.

Researchers have developed **edible** **packaging** for food.

99 PERCENT
OF MICROBE SPECIES HAVE NOT YET BEEN DISCOVERED, SCIENTISTS ESTIMATE.

THE SIZE OF A LARGE PIZZA, THE **COIN** WEIGHS **220 POUNDS.**

(100 kg)

CANADA HAS PRODUCED A MILLION-DOLLAR COIN.

City bees pollinate more plants than **country bees** do, a study found.

IN SPAIN, THE TOOTH **FAIRY** IS A **MOUSE** NAMED **PÉREZ.**

Pumpkins are 90 percent water.

SCIENTISTS MADE TEMPORARY TATTOOS THAT CAN BE USED TO CONTROL SMARTPHONES.

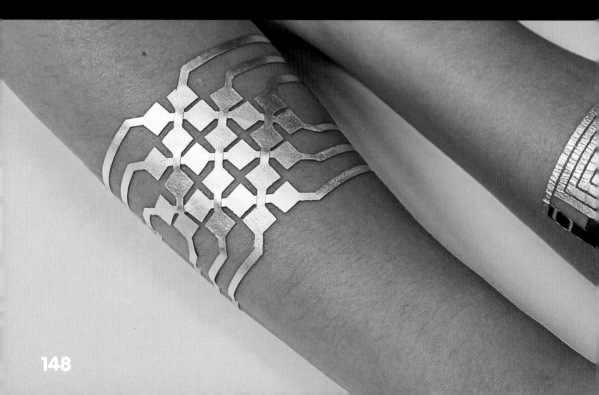

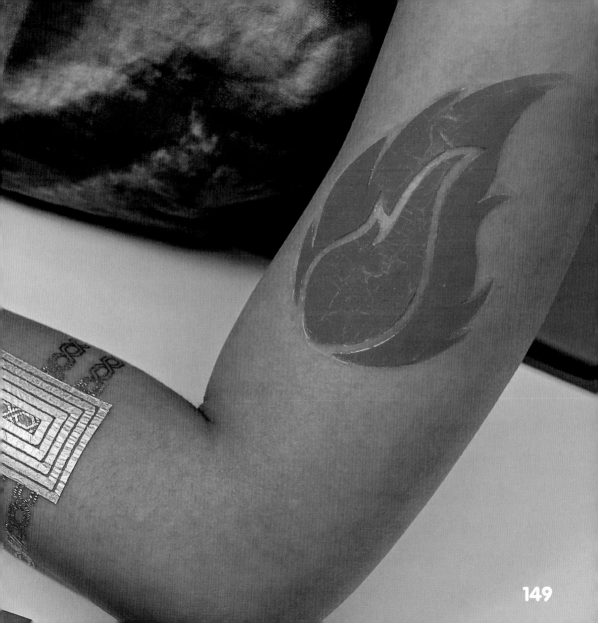

A **cat** once co-authored a **physics paper.**

SOME ANCIENT MUMMIES HAVE BEEN FOUND WITH MUMMIFIED HEAD LICE.

THERE IS AN ASTEROID SHAPED LIKE A DOG BONE.

Some trees know when their branches have been nibbled by an animal.

SCIENTISTS DISCOVERED A **NEW SPIDER** SPECIES THAT **LOOKS LIKE A** DRIED-UP **LEAF.**

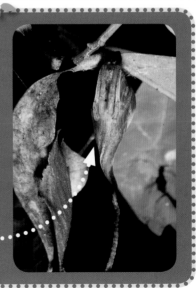

There's a huge heart-shaped ice patch on the surface of Pluto.

THAT'S WEIRD!

Baby hedgehogs are called hoglets.

Coral reef–dwelling **fish** can see **colors** that humans can't.

Hot, dry weather caused piles of **horse poop** to **burst into flames** outside a **stable** in upstate New York, U.S.A.

THE POLICE HEADQUARTERS KNOWN AS **SCOTLAND YARD** IS NOT IN **SCOTLAND.**

Female donkeys are called **jennys.** Males are called **jacks.**

Scientists built an engine small enough to fit inside a **human cell.**

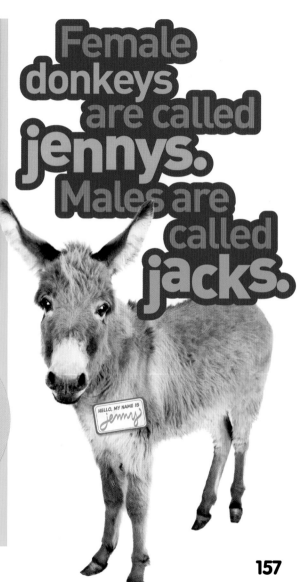

HELLO, MY NAME IS *Jenny*

U.S. PRESIDENT GEORGE WASHINGTON NEVER LIVED IN THE WHITE HOUSE.

IN BOTH 1841 AND 1881 THERE WERE THREE U.S. PRESIDENTS IN ONE YEAR.

THERE'S A FLOWER SHOP, A CHOCOLATE SHOP, AND A BOWLING ALLEY IN THE WHITE HOUSE BASEMENT.

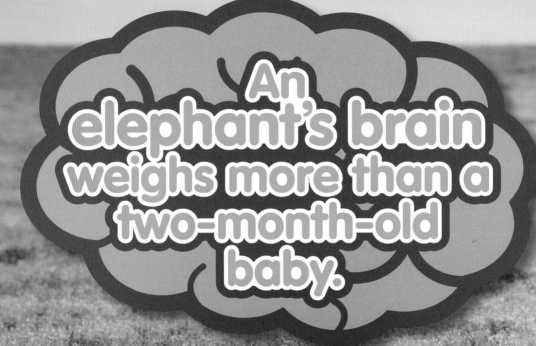

An elephant's brain weighs more than a two-month-old baby.

WATER BEETLES MAKE **HOMES** IN ELEPHANT FOOTPRINTS.

A **pet dog** named Keon **has a record-setting tail** that's as long as a **skateboard.**

Q is the only **letter** of the alphabet that does not appear in the **name** of any **U.S. state.**

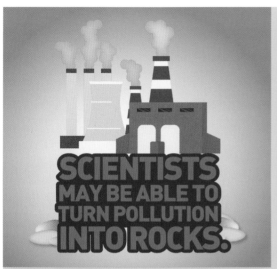

SCIENTISTS MAY BE ABLE TO TURN POLLUTION INTO ROCKS.

Some dinosaurs **quacked** like **ducks**, according to a recent study.

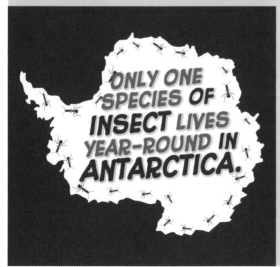

ONLY ONE SPECIES OF INSECT LIVES YEAR-ROUND IN ANTARCTICA.

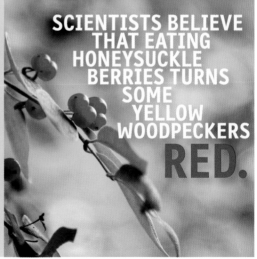

SCIENTISTS BELIEVE THAT EATING HONEYSUCKLE BERRIES TURNS SOME YELLOW WOODPECKERS RED.

AN **EXHIBIT** AT THE AMERICAN MUSEUM OF NATURAL HISTORY IN NEW YORK CITY USED **MODERN IMAGING TECHNOLOGY** TO SHOW VISITORS **WHAT MUMMIES REALLY LOOKED** LIKE UNDER THEIR **WRAPPINGS.**

SEA OTTERS—which use rocks to open shellfish—may have been using tools **BEFORE HUMANS EVEN EXISTED.**

POTATO CHIPS SOLD FOR MORE THAN **$12 A BAG—** SIX TIMES THEIR REGULAR PRICE— DURING A 2017 POTATO SHORTAGE **IN JAPAN.**

SCIENTISTS **INVENTED A PAIR OF GLASSES** THAT ALLOWS THE WEARER TO **SEE COLORS** THAT ARE NORMALLY INVISIBLE TO THE HUMAN EYE.

DINOSAUR FOOTPRINTS DISCOVERED IN AUSTRALIA IN 2017 ARE **5.6 FEET** (1.7 M) **LONG—** THE **LARGEST EVER FOUND.**

A RETIRED GERMAN STATISTICIAN **SOLVED A MATH PROBLEM** THAT HAS **STUMPED EXPERTS** SINCE THE 1950S—WHILE **BRUSHING** HIS **TEETH.**

GIANT NEW ZEALAND PARROTS CALLED **KEAS** MAKE EACH OTHER **"LAUGH."**

SCIENTISTS THINK A HUGE ASTEROID MAY HAVE SMASHED INTO SATURN'S MOON **ENCELADUS,** CREATING ICE VOLCANOES ON ITS SURFACE.

A new species of SHRIMP was named *SYNALPHEUS PINKFLOYDI* after the rock band PINK FLOYD.

SOME BIRDS **"HIGH-FIVE"** IN MIDAIR.

RATS **"GIGGLE"** WHEN **TICKLED,** A STUDY FOUND.

That's Weird!

A man in Florida, U.S.A., robbed a farmers market while wearing **a tutu.**

AT A CONTEST IN SLOVAKIA, **GRAVE DIGGERS** GO SHOVEL TO SHOVEL TO SEE WHO CAN DIG THE FASTEST— AND TIDIEST— **GRAVE.**

Catfish whiskers are known as **barbels.**

There's a **contest** to come up with the **worst sound** in the **world.**

Submissions included the sounds of **chili being stirred** and **nails** on a chalkboard.

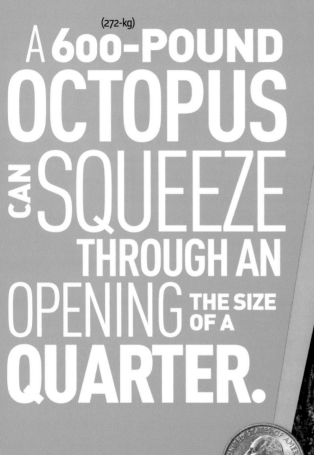

A **600-POUND** (272-kg) **OCTOPUS** can **SQUEEZE** THROUGH AN **OPENING** THE SIZE OF A **QUARTER.**

SCIENTISTS NICKNAMED A PATCH OF UNUSUALLY WARM PACIFIC OCEAN WATER "THE BLOB."

170

Cookie Monster said his name used to be Sid.

Scientists found a huge **lake** under a **volcano** in Bolivia.

SOME **BIRDS' BEAKS HAVE BUILT-IN AIR CONDITIONERS.**

A giant anteater flicks its tongue in and out of its mouth up to 150 times per minute.

HAPPY COWS MAKE MORE NUTRITIOUS MILK.

SOME SNAILS HIT PREDATORS WITH THEIR SHELLS.

SOME SCORPIONS HAVE 12 EYES.

An **ice-cream shop** in England is testing using a **drone** to deliver its **treats** to customers.

Nine-banded armadillos almost always give birth to **identical quadruplets.**

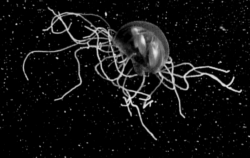

Scientists recently discovered a **jellyfish** that looks like a **glowing UFO.**

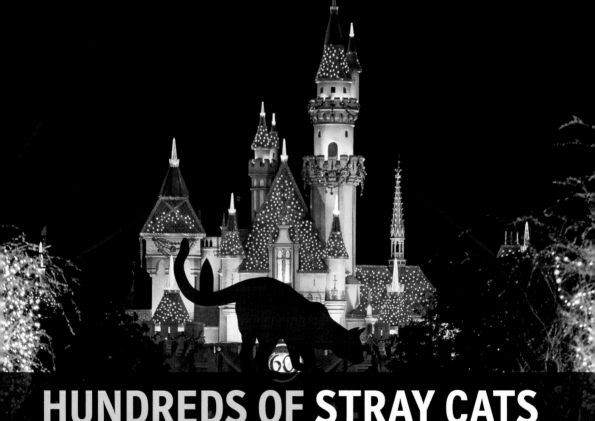

HUNDREDS OF STRAY CATS ROAM AROUND DISNEYLAND, IN CALIFORNIA, U.S.A., AT NIGHT TO CATCH **REAL-LIFE MICE.**

A large green snake stowed away on a plane flying to Mexico City.

A **TEEN** IN WASHINGTON STATE, U.S.A., ONCE GOT HER **HEAD** STUCK INSIDE A GIANT **PUMPKIN.**

DON'T TRY THIS AT HOME!

THE **SKIN** OF ONE KIND OF SMALL AMAZONIAN **FROG** IS COVERED WITH **ANT** REPELLENT.

PLANTS MAY GROW FASTER IF YOU PLAY MUSIC FOR THEM.

YOU CAN
EAT
A MEAL

IN AN
AIRPLANE-
THEMED
RESTAURANT—

INSIDE
AN ACTUAL
PLANE—
IN WUHAN, CHINA.

LILY AIRWAYS BAR

THE FIRST WOMAN TO RUN FOR U.S. PRESIDENT RAN BEFORE WOMEN COULD VOTE.

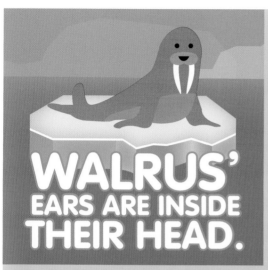

WALRUS'
EARS ARE INSIDE
THEIR HEAD.

Fireflies in the western United States don't glow.

#JINGLEJOHNS

AN INDIANA, U.S.A., COMPANY DESIGNED **PORTABLE TOILETS** THAT LIGHT UP AND SING **CHRISTMAS CAROLS.**

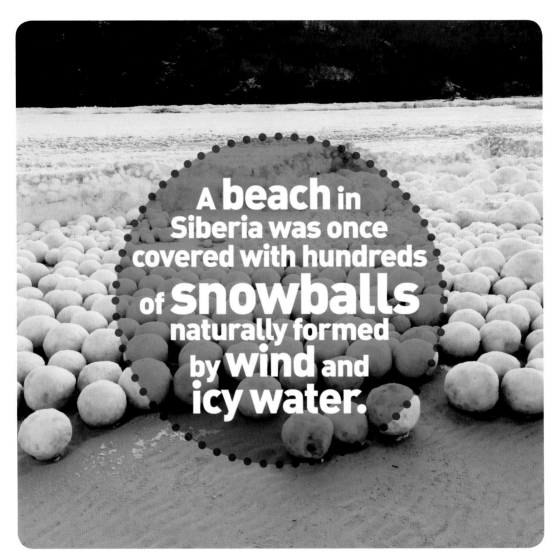

A **beach** in Siberia was once covered with hundreds of **snowballs** naturally formed by **wind** and **icy water.**

Civil War–era **cannonballs** washed up on a South Carolina, U.S.A., **beach** after a hurricane.

IT COULD TAKE
300 years
TO DISCOVER EVERY SPECIES OF

tree IN THE
Amazon rain forest.

Some birds use "baby talk" when singing to chicks.

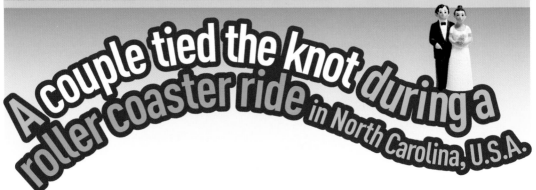

A couple tied the knot during a roller coaster ride in North Carolina, U.S.A.

Each year, Americans throw away some $60 million in loose change.

Only 8 percent of U.S. money is paper and coins (the rest is just numbers on a computer).

A NEW YORK MAN CREATED A **VIDEO-GAME-THEMED HALLOWEEN COSTUME** THAT PLAYS AN ACTUAL VIDEO GAME.

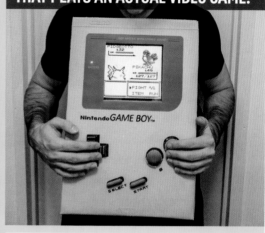

A **HUNTSMAN SPIDER** CAN GROW AS BIG AS A **DINNER PLATE.**

GORILLAS CAN CATCH HUMAN COLDS.

FISH CALLED SKATES CAN SEE ONLY IN BLACK AND WHITE.

U.S. PRESIDENT BARACK OBAMA ONCE WORKED AT AN ICE-CREAM SHOP.

YOU CAN ORDER SCOOPS OF PEAR-AND-BLUE-CHEESE-FLAVORED ICE CREAM AT A SHOP IN PORTLAND, OREGON, U.S.A.

ASPARAGUS, OYSTER, AND PARMESAN CHEESE WERE POPULAR ICE-CREAM FLAVORS IN THE UNITED STATES IN THE 18TH CENTURY.

An **Italian man** piled **121 scoops** of ice cream onto one cone.

A **hotel** in the Grand Canyon Caverns is 220 feet underground.

(67 m)

Northern stargazer fish zap their predators with a jolt of electricity.

Road **noise** from nearby **highways** can make it hard for some animals to **sniff out** predators.

A FOSSIL HUNTER IN THE U.K. FOUND A "**PICKLED**" DINOSAUR BRAIN.

THOUSANDS OF YEARS AGO, SOME PEOPLE CARRIED WATER AROUND IN HOLLOWED **OSTRICH EGGS.**

MICE CAN FEEL EACH **other's pain.**

A **FLOCK** OF **FLYING** **WiLD** TURKEYS CAUSED POWER OUTAGES IN AN OREGON, U.S.A., TOWN.

DUNG BEETLES TAKE MENTAL "SNAPSHOTS" OF THE NIGHT SKY.

wheee!

Warty Goblin, Cinderella, and Wee-B-Little are all types of **pumpkins.**

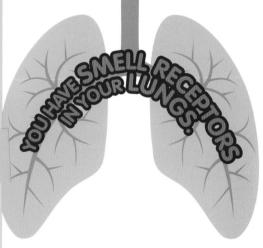

YOU HAVE SMELL RECEPTORS IN YOUR LUNGS.

Dogs in the U.K. were trained to **fly** an **airplane.**

SOME DINOSAURS HAD FOREST-CAMOUFLAGE COLORING.

THE FIRST MODERN COMPUTER WEIGHED 30 TONS.
(27 t)

THAT'S HEAVY!

THE FIRST CELL PHONE, NICKNAMED "THE BRICK," WEIGHED TWO POUNDS. (0.9 kg)

RESEARCHERS FOUND THAT RATS THAT LISTENED TO MOZART LEARNED TO RUN MAZES FASTER THAN RATS THAT LISTENED TO OTHER MUSIC.

SOME FROG CALLS CAN BE HEARD UP TO A MILE AWAY.

(1.6 km)

A baby echidna is called a puggle.

TREES "SLEEP" AT NIGHT.

Tadpoles eat **vegetarian meals** during heat waves.

RESEARCHERS HAVE FOUND A WAY TO **USE** SEWAGE TO **MAKE** FUEL.

Dog fleas **jump** higher than cat fleas.

U.S. TOWNS AND CITIES WITH THE

Good Grief, Idaho

IDAHO

SOUTH DAKOTA

Plenty Bears, South Dakota

CALIFORNIA

Zzzyzx, California

TEXAS

Ding Dong, Texas

STRANGEST NAMES INCLUDE...

Goobertown, Arkansas

Lizard Lick, North Carolina

Boar Tush, Alabama

NORTH CAROLINA

ARKANSAS

ALABAMA

GUESS WHAT?

J is actually the last letter of the alphabet!
HOW?

It looks light and fluffy, but it weighs as much as 100 elephants!
WHAT?

Some chickens wear sweaters!
WHERE?

WANNA FIND OUT?

The FUN doesn't have to end here! Find these far-out facts and more in *Weird But True! 10.*

FACTFINDER

Boldface indicates illustrations.

FACTFINDER

G

Garbage trucks 118, **118**
Geese 80, **80**
Genes 27, 84
Giant anteaters 171, **171**
Giant Pacific octopuses 135, **135**
Giant pandas 45, **45**, 125, **125**
Ginsburg, Ruth Bader 115
Giraffes 132, **132**
Glass harmonica 52, **52**
Glasses 164
Glow-in-the-dark bands **86–87**, 87
Glow-in-the-dark sidewalks 6
Glowing purple blob 56, **56**
Goats 41, **41**
Gold coin 146, **146**
Gold doughnut 133, **133**
Gold medals, Olympic 19, **19**
Gold toilet 36, **36**
Goobertown, Arkansas, U.S.A. 207
Good Grief, Idaho, U.S.A. 206
Good luck 27, **27**
Gorillas 22, **22–23**, 190, **190**
GPS: in cockroaches 61
Grand Canyon and Caverns, Arizona, U.S.A. 71, 194, **194**
Grave-digging contest 166
Great frigate birds 72, **72–73**
Great Wall of China, China 44, **44**
Green Bank, West Virginia, U.S.A. 144, **144**
Guinea pigs 94, **94**, 129, **129**
Gut microbes 108

H

Hagfish slime 124
Halloween costumes 189, **189**
Harmonica, glass 52, **52**
Harry Potter and the Philosopher's Stone (Rowling) 6, **6**
Hawaii, U.S.A. 58, 62, **62**
Head lice, mummified 144
Hedgehogs 153, **153**
Hermit crabs **142–143**, 143
Highway noise 195
Hoglets 153, **153**
Honeybees 140, **140**
Honeysuckle berries 163, **163**
Hornets 7
Horses 91, **91**, 156
Hotels 15, **15**, 24, **24**, 194, **194**
House: in aircraft hangar 48, **48–49**
Hoverbikes 84
Human body
    genes 27
    gut microbes 108
    lungs 197, **197**
    parts 107, **107**
    teeth 106, **106**, 124, **124**
    3-D printing 47, **47**
    yawning **116–117**, 117
Human settlements, ancient 43
Huntsman spiders 189

I

Ice cream 51, **51**, 173, **173**, 192–193, **192–193**
Ice hotel 15, **15**

Ice volcanoes 165
Insects: in Antarctica 163
Insomnia 115
Io (moon) 84, **84**
Ireland 68–69, **68–69**

J

Jackals 136, **136–137**
Jeans 139, **139**
Jellyfish 76, **76**, 125, **125**, 176, **176**
Jupiter (planet) 84

K

Kangaroos 88, **88**
Keas 165, **165**
Kenya: power outage 108
Ketchup 51, **51**
Koalas 45, **45**
Kryptonite 10, **10**

L

Lakes 130, **130–131**, 171
Leatherback turtles 125
Left-handedness 88
Legs, hearing with 133
Lenses 84
Leonardo da Vinci 42
Libraries 25, **25**, 62
Lice, mummified 150, **150**
Lightning 133
Lizard Lick, North Carolina, U.S.A. 207
Lungs 197, **197**

FACTFINDER

FACTFINDER

PHOTO CREDITS

Since 1888, the National Geographic Society has funded more than 12,000 research, exploration, and preservation projects around the world. The Society receives funds from National Geographic Partners, LLC, funded in part by your purchase. A portion of the proceeds from this book supports this vital work. To learn more, visit natgeo.com/info.

For more information, visit nationalgeographic.com, call 1-800-647-5463, or write to the following address:

National Geographic Partners
1145 17th Street N.W.
Washington, D.C. 20036-4688 U.S.A.

Visit us online at nationalgeographic.com/books

For librarians and teachers:
ngchildrensbooks.org

More for kids from National Geographic:
kids.nationalgeographic.com

For information about special discounts for bulk purchases, please contact National Geographic Books Special Sales: specialsales@natgeo.com

For rights or permissions inquiries, please contact National Geographic Books Subsidiary Rights: bookrights@natgeo.com

Designed by Rachael Hamm Plett, Moduza Design

First edition published 2017
Reissued and updated 2018

Trade paperback ISBN: 978-1-4263-3120-6
Reinforced library binding ISBN: 978-1-4263-3121-3

The publisher would like to thank Jen Agresta, project editor; Avery Hurt, researcher; Sarah Wassner Flynn, researcher; Stephanie Drimmer, researcher; Paige Towler, project manager; Julide Dengel, art director; Kathryn Robbins; art director; Lori Epstein, photo director; Hillary Leo, photo editor; Molly Reid, production editor; Gus Tello and Anne LeongSon, production assistants.

Printed in China
18/PPS/1